国际财务报告准则

国际会计准则第27号
——单独财务报表

（汉英对照）

中国会计准则委员会　组织翻译

中国财政经济出版社

图书在版编目（CIP）数据

国际会计准则．第27号，单独财务报表：汉、英/中国会计准则委员会组织翻译．北京：中国财政经济出版社，2012.12

（国际财务报告准则）

ISBN 978-7-5095-4149-4

Ⅰ．①国… Ⅱ．①中… Ⅲ．①国际会计准则-汉、英 Ⅳ．①F233．1

中国版本图书馆CIP数据核字（2012）第287510号

责任编辑：樊清玉　　版式设计：康普宝蓝

封面设计：九州迅驰

中国财政经济出版社出版

URL：http：//ckfz.cfeph.cn

E-mail：ckfz@cfeph.cn

社址：北京市海淀区阜成路甲28号　邮政编码：100142

发行处电话：88190406　财经书店电话：64033436

河北零五印刷厂印刷　各地新华书店经销

787×1092毫米　16开　3印张　60 000字

2013年1月第1版　2013年1月河北第1次印刷

定价：16.00元

ISBN 978-7-5095-4149-4/F·3369

（图书出现印装问题，本社负责调换）

图字：01-2013-0577

本社质量投诉电话：010-88190744

International Financial Reporting Standards (IFRSs) together with their accompanying documents are issued by the International Accounting Standards Board (IASB):

30 Cannon Street, London, EC4M 6XH, United Kingdom.

Tel: +44 (0) 20 7246 6410 Fax: +44 (0) 20 7246 6411

Email: info@ifrs.org Web: www.ifrs.org

ISBN 978-7-5095-4149-4

IFRS Foundation Publications Department

30 Cannon Street, London, EC4M 6XH, United Kingdom.

Tel: +44 (0) 20 7332 2730 Fax: +44 (0) 20 7332 2749

Email: publications@ifrs.org Web: www.ifrs.org

国际财务报告准则（IFRSs）及其配套文件由国际会计准则理事会（IASB）发布。
30 Cannon Street, London, EC4M 6XH, United Kingdom.
Tel: +44 (0) 20 7246 6410　Fax: +44 (0) 20 7246 6411
Email: info@ifrs.org
Web: www.ifrs.org

ISBN 978-7-5095-4149-4

IFRS Foundation Publications Department
30 Cannon Street, London, EC4M 6XH, United Kingdom.
Tel: +44 (0) 20 7332 2730　Fax: +44 (0) 20 7332 2749
Email: publications@ifrs.org　Web: www.ifrs.org

国际财务报告准则中文翻译审核专家组

组　长： 王　军　财政部党组副书记、副部长，中国会计准则委员会主席，博士生导师

副组长： 余蔚平　财政部部长助理

组　员： 冯淑萍　全国人大常委会预算工作委员会副主任，中国会计准则委员会委员，博士生导师

沈小南　全国社会保障基金理事会副理事长，中国会计准则委员会咨询专家

杨　敏　财政部会计司司长，中国会计准则委员会秘书长

汤云为　上海财经大学教授，上海市会计学会会长，博士生导师

刘光忠　财政部会计司副司长，中国会计学会秘书长

袁文辉　德勤华永会计师事务所技术部合伙人，中国会计准则委员会咨询专家

支晓强　中国人民大学商学院副院长，副教授

毛新述　北京工商大学商学院副院长，副教授

陆建桥　财政部会计司准则二处处长，中国会计准则委员会咨询专家

出版说明

2011年，国际会计准则理事会先后发布了《国际财务报告准则第10号——合并财务报表》、《国际财务报告准则第11号——合营安排》、《国际财务报告准则第12号——在其他主体中权益的披露》和《国际财务报告准则第13号——公允价值计量》四项新准则，并对《国际会计准则第1号——财务报表列报》、《国际会计准则第19号——雇员福利》、《国际会计准则第27号——合并财务报表和单独财务报表》和《国际会计准则第28号——在联营企业和合营企业中的投资》四项准则进行了修订。除修订后的《国际会计准则第1号》于2012年7月1日生效外，上述其他新发布或修订的国际财务报告准则都将于2013年1月1日起生效。

我国2006年发布的企业会计准则体系实现了与国际财务报告准则的趋同。2010年，财政部又发布了《中国企业会计准则与国际财务报告准则持续趋同路线图》。为借鉴国际财务报告准则完善我国企业会计准则体系，实现中国准则与国际财务报告准则的持续趋同，中国会计准则委员会组织人员对国际会计准则理事会新发布或修订的上述八项准则进行了翻译。经国际财务报告准则基金会认可的中文翻译审核专家组审核，上述国际财务报告准则中文版是国际财务报告准则基金会认可的国际财务报告准则官方译本，为国际财务报告准则基金会的正式出版物。

在翻译审校过程中，财政部会计司陆建桥、高大平、朱琳、陈瑜、夏文贤、徐华新、林屾等同志对本书的译稿进行了校译。财政部会计司副司长、中国会计学会秘书长刘光忠和财政部会计司司长、中国会计准则委员会秘书长杨敏对全部译稿进行了审阅。本书最后由财政部部长助理余蔚平和财政部党组副书记、副部长、中国会计准则委员会主席王军审定。值此相关国际财务报告准则中文版出版之际，特别感谢国际财务报告准则中文翻译审核专家组以及中国财政经济出版社的有关同志为本书的翻译出版工作所付出的辛勤劳动！

中国会计准则委员会

2013 年 1 月

目 录

引言

1 《国际会计准则第 27 号——单独财务报表》包括主体编制单独财务报表时对子公司、合营企业和联营企业投资的会计处理和披露要求。本准则要求编制单独财务报表的主体以成本或按照《国际财务报告准则第 9 号——金融工具》对此类投资进行会计处理。

2 本准则自 2013 年 1 月 1 日或以后日期开始的年度期间起生效。允许提前采用。

国际财务报告准则第27号
——单独财务报表

目标

1. 本准则的目标是规范主体在编制单独财务报表时对子公司、合营企业和联营企业投资的会计处理和披露要求。

范围

2. 当主体选择或当地监管要求主体编制单独财务报表时，本准则适用于对子公司、合营企业和联营企业投资的会计处理。

3. 本准则不规定哪些主体提供单独财务报表。当主体编制遵循国际财务报告准则的单独财务报表时，应适用本准则。

定义

4. 本准则中使用的以下术语的含义是：

合并财务报表，指集团的财务报表，在该报表中母公司及其子公司的资产、负债、权益、收入、费用和现金流量都按单一经济主体编报。

单独财务报表，是指由母公司（即控制子公司的投资者）或对被投资者具有共同控制或重大影响的投资者编制的财务报表，在该报表中投资都以成本或按《国际财务报告准则第9号——金融工具》处理。

5. 以下术语在《国际财务报告准则第10号——合并财务报表》的附录一、《国际财务报告准则第11号——合营安排》的附录一以及《国际会计准则第28号——

在联营企业和合营企业中的投资》第3段中予以定义。

- 联营企业
- 控制被投资者
- 集团
- 共同控制
- 合营企业
- 合营企业者
- 母公司
- 重大影响
- 子公司

6. 除第8段列举的情况外，单独财务报表是合并财务报表或者采用权益法核算联营企业或合营企业中投资的财务报表之外编制的报表。单独财务报表无需附在这些报表之后。

7. 采用权益法的财务报表不是单独财务报表。相似地，没有子公司以及联营企业或合营企业中投资的主体的财务报表也不是单独财务报表。

8. 根据《国际财务报告准则第10号》第4段（1）豁免编制合并财务报表和根据《国际会计准则第28号》（2011年修改）第17段免于应用权益法的主体可以编制单独财务报表作为其唯一的财务报表。

编制单独财务报表

9. 除第10段外，单独财务报表的编制应遵循所有适用的国际财务报告准则。

10. 主体编制单独财务报表时，对在子公司、合营企业和联营企业中的投资应采用以下方法核算：

（1）成本，或者

（2）按照《国际财务报告准则第9号》的规定。

主体应对每一类投资适用相同的会计处理方法。以成本核算的投资被分类为持有待售时（或包括在分类为持有待售的处置组中），应适用《国际财务报告准则第5号——持有待售的非流动资产和终止经营》的要求。在此类情况下，按照《国际财务报告准则第9号》规定核算的投资无需作调整。

11. 根据《国际会计准则第28号》（2011年修改）第18段，如果主体选择按照《国际财务报告准则第9号》的要求，对联营企业或合营企业中的投资以公允价值计量且其变动计入损益，在单独财务报表中应采用相同的方法对这类投资进行会计处理。

12. 对于子公司、合营企业与联营企业的股利，主体应在取得收取股利的权利时在单独财务报表中将其确认为损益。

13. 当母公司通过设立新的主体作为其母公司对集团进行结构重组时，如果符合下列条件：

（1）新的母公司通过发行权益工具交换原母公司的权益工具来获得对原母公司的控制；

（2）在重组前后，新集团和原集团的资产和负债相同；以及

（3）重组前原母公司的所有者对重组前后原集团和新集团的净资产具有相同的绝对和相对权益。

并且，在单独财务报表中新母公司根据第10段（1）的规定核算其对原母公司的投资，新母公司应以重组日原母公司单独财务报表中享有权益项份额的账面价值作为对原母公司投资的账面成本。

14. 类似地，不是母公司的主体可能采用符合第13段条件的方式设立新主体作为其母公司。第13段的要求同样适用于这类重组。在这类情形下，"原母公司"和"原集团"都指的是"原主体"。

披露

15. 在单独财务报表中进行披露时，主体应当应用所有适用的国际财务报告准则，包括第16段和17段的要求。

16. 当主体根据《国际财务报告准则第10号》第4段（1）的规定，选择不编制合并财务报表，而是编制单独财务报表时，应当在单独财务报表中披露：

（1）财务报表是单独财务报表的事实；适用了豁免编制合并财务报表的条款；遵循国际财务报告准则编制供公开使用的合并财务报表主体的名称和主要业务地点（和注册国家，如果不同的话）；可获取这些合并财务报表的地址。

（2）在子公司、合营企业和联营企业中的重大投资的清单，包括：

①被投资者的名称。

②被投资者业务的主要地点（和注册国家，如果不同的话）。

③持有的权益占被投资者所有权比例（和表决权比例，如果不同的话）。

（3）描述对（2）中列举的投资采用的核算方法。

17. 当母公司（除第16段涵盖的母公司外）或对被投资者具有共同控制或重大影响的投资者编制单独财务报表时，母公司或投资者应指出与其相关的按照《国际财务报告准则第10号》、《国际财务报告准则第11号》或《国际会计准则第28号》（2011年修改）编制的财务报表。母公司或投资者还应当在其单独财务报表中披露：

（1）该报表是单独财务报表的事实以及编制该报表的原因，如果法律并不要求编制。

（2）在子公司、合营企业与联营企业中的重大投资的清单，包括：

①被投资者的名称。

②被投资者的主要业务地点（和注册国家，如果不同的话）。

③持有的权益占被投资者所有权比例（和表决权比例，如果不同的话）。

(3) 描述对 (2) 中列举的投资采用的核算方法。

生效日期和过渡性规定

18. 主体应当在 2013 年 1 月 1 日或以后日期开始的年度期间采用本准则。允许提前采用。如果提前采用本准则，主体应披露这一事实，并同时适用《国际财务报告准则第 10 号》、《国际财务报告准则第 11 号》和《国际财务报告准则第 12 号——在其他主体中权益的披露》以及《国际会计准则第 28 号》(2011 年修改)。

参考《国际财务报告准则第 9 号》

19. 如果主体采用本准则但尚未采用《国际财务报告准则第 9 号》，任何对《国际财务报告准则第 9 号》的参考应视为参考《国际会计准则第 39 号——金融工具：确认和计量》。

撤销《国际会计准则第 27 号》(2008 年)

20. 本准则与《国际财务报告准则第 10 号》同时发布。这两项准则取代了《国际会计准则第 27 号——合并财务报表和单独财务报表》(2008 年修改)。

理事会批准 2003 年 12 月发布的《国际会计准则第 27 号》

国际会计准则理事会 14 位理事中的 13 位同意批准发布《国际会计准则第 27 号——合并财务报表和单独财务报表》(2003 年修订)。Yamada 先生不同意。他关于合并财务报表的反对意见列示在《国际财务报告准则第 10 号——合并财务报表》结论基础之后。

David Tweedie 爵士	主席
Thomas E Jones	副主席
Mary E Barth	
Hans-Georg Bruns	
Anthony T Cope	
Robert P Garnett	
Gilbert Gélard	
James J Leisenring	
Warren J McGregor	
Patricia L O'Malley	
Harry K Schmid	
John T Smith	
Geoffrey Whittington	
Tatsumi Yamada	

理事会批准 2008 年 5 月发布的《在子公司、共同控制主体或联营企业中的投资的成本》（对《国际财务报告准则第 1 号》和《国际会计准则第 27 号》的修改）

国际会计准则理事会 13 位理事中的 11 位同意批准发布《在子公司、共同控制主体或联营企业中的投资的成本》（对《国际财务报告准则第 1 号——首次采用国际财务报告准则》和《国际会计准则第 27 号》的修改）。Barth 教授和 Danjou 先生不同意。他们的不同意见列示在结论基础之后。

David Tweedie 爵士　　主席
Thomas E Jones　　副主席
Mary E Barth
Stephen Cooper
Philippe Danjou
Jan Engström
Robert P Garnett
Gilbert Gélard
James J Leisenring
Warren J McGregor
John T Smith
Tatsumi Yamada
Wei-Guo Zhang

《国际会计准则第 27 号——单独财务报表》结论基础

本结论基础与《国际会计准则第 27 号》一并发布，但不属于其组成部分。

引言

1. 本结论基础概述了国际会计准则理事会在 2003 年发布《国际会计准则第 27 号——合并财务报表和单独财务报表》，以及在 2008 年、2011 年对其进行修改时，形成结论过程中所考虑的因素。理事会理事个人对有些因素比对其他因素更为重视。除非特别说明，以下对《国际会计准则第 27 号》的参考，都是指本准则之前的版本。

2. 2011 年对《国际会计准则第 27 号》的修改源于理事会关于合并财务报表准则的项目。一项新的国际财务报告准则，即《国际财务报告准则第 10 号——合并财务报表》明确了与合并财务报表编制相关的控制原则和要求。因此，目前的《国际会计准则第 27 号》仅包括与单独财务报表有关的要求。本准则修改后的标题——单独财务报表，反映了这一变化。

3. 2011 年，理事会在批准发布《国际财务报告准则第 10 号》时，也批准了对《国际会计准则第 27 号》所做的相应修改，在本准则中删除了与合并财务报表相关的所有要求。

4. 同时，理事会将《国际会计准则第 28 号——联营企业中的投资》和《国际会计准则第 31 号——合营企业中的权益》中关于单独财务报表的要求移入到《国际会计准则第 27 号》中。这些要求见本准则的第 6 段至 8 段。考虑到删除和移入的内容，理事会决定对修改后《国际会计准则第 27 号》的段落重新编号。本准则中的定义和术语也相应进行了更新，以与《国际财务报告准则第 10 号》、《国际财务报告准则第 11 号——合营企业安排》、《国际财务报告准则第 12 号——在其他主体中权益的披露》和《国际会计准则第 28 号——在联营企业和合营企业中的投资》的要求保持一致。

5. 2003 年发布《国际会计准则第 27 号》时，也一并发布了结论基础，概述了理事会当时形成结论过程中考虑的因素。该结论基础随后也相应进行了更新，以反映对本准则的修改。

6. 目前的结论基础仅包括理事会就单独财务报表所作的考虑。交叉索引相应作了更新，同时也作了一些细微必要的编辑修改。关于就合并财务报表讨论的段落相应地移入《国际财务报告准则第 10 号》的结论基础中。

非公众主体豁免编制合并财务报表

7. 理事会决定，满足《国际财务报告准则第 10 号》第 4 段（1）条件，免于编制合并财务报表的母公司，应当在其单独财务报表中采用与其他母公司、在合营企业中拥有权益的合营企业者或联营企业的投资者，在它们单独财务报表核算其投资相一致的方法，对子公司投资进行会计处理。理事会明确区分了对此类投资作为权益投资的会计处理与对母公司控制的经济主体的会计处理。对于前者，理事会决定每一类投资都应采取一致的方法进行会计处理。

8. 理事会决定，单独财务报表中对投资的会计处理应采用相同的方法，无论其编制时的情况如何。因此，编制合并财务报表的母公司与因豁免而不编制合并财务报表的母公司都应编制相同形式的单独财务报表。

单独财务报表中对子公司、合营企业和联营企业投资的计量（2003 年修订和 2008 年修改）

9.《国际会计准则第 27 号》（理事会的前身在 2000 年的修订版）允许在母公司单独财务报表中，对子公司投资采用三种方法中的任何一种来计量。这三种方法是：成本法、权益法或者按照《国际会计准则第 39 号——金融工具：确认和计量》[①] 作为可供出售金融资产[②]计量。《国际会计准则第 28 号——在联营企业中的投资》允许单独财务报表中对在联营企业中的投资采用同样的选择，并且《国际会计准则第 31 号——合营中的权益》合营企业者单独财务报表中对在合营企业中的权益没有倾向任何特定会计处理。但是，理事会在 2003 年决定，要求所有包含在单独财务报表中的投资采用成本法或按照《国际会计准则第 39 号》进行会计处理，不再将权益法作

① 2009 年 11 月和 2010 年 10 月，国际会计准则理事会修改了《国际会计准则第 39 号》的一些要求，并将它们移入《国际财务报告准则第 9 号——金融工具》。《国际财务报告准则第 9 号》适用于所有纳入《国际会计准则第 39 号》范围的项目。

② 2009 年 11 月发布、2010 年 10 月修改的《国际财务报告准则第 9 号——金融工具》删除了可供出售类资产这一类别。

为可供选择的计量方法。

10. 尽管权益法可能为使用者提供一些类似于通过合并得到的损益的信息，但理事会注意到，这些信息已反映在投资者的合并或个别财务报表中，并且不需要提供给单独财务报表使用者。对于单独财务报表而言，重点应集中反映作为投资的资产的业绩。理事会的结论认为，不管是按照《国际会计准则第 39 号》[①] 采用公允价值法还是采用成本法编制的单独财务报表都具有相关性。按照《国际会计准则第 39 号》采用公允价值计量能够提供投资的经济价值信息。使用成本法也能够得到相关的信息，这取决于编制单独财务报表的目的。例如，可能只有特定方需要单独财务报表以确定来自子公司的股利收入。

11. 作为 2007 年开始的年度改进项目的一部分，理事会确认了一项与《国际财务报告准则第 5 号——持有待售的非流动资产和终止经营》明显不一致之处。如果适用《国际会计准则第 39 号》的投资根据《国际财务报告准则第 5 号》的要求分类为持有待售，该不一致与母公司在其单独财务报表的会计处理相关。第 10 段要求编制单独财务报表的主体对于分类为持有待售的投资（或者包含在分类为持有待售的处置组中）按照《国际财务报告准则第 5 号》进行会计处理，如果该投资以成本法核算。然而，主体按照《国际会计准则第 39 号》进行会计处理的金融资产被排除在《国际财务报告准则第 5 号》的计量要求之外。

12. 《国际财务报告准则第 5 号》结论基础第 13 段指出，理事会决定，非流动资产只有符合以下条件时才排除在《国际财务报告准则第 5 号》的计量范围之外：（1）以公允价值计量且其变动计入损益；（2）其公允价值减出售费用难以确定。[②] 理事会在《国际财务报告准则第 5 号》的结论基础中承认，并不是《国际会计准则第 39 号》范围内的所有金融资产都以公允价值计量且其变动计入损益，但是理事会当时并不计划对金融资产的会计处理作任何修改。

13. 因此，理事会通过 2008 年 5 月发布的《对国际财务报告准则的改进》修改了第 10 段，使在单独财务报表中对此类投资按照《国际会计准则第 39 号》的要求进行的处理，与《国际财务报告准则第 5 号》为分类为持有待售之前根据《国际会计准则第 39 号》进行会计处理的其他资产提供的计量范围排除要求保持一致。因此，如果此类投资满足《国际财务报告准则第 5 号》关于持有待售的条件，主体应当继续根据《国际会计准则第 39 号》对此类投资进行会计处理。

从子公司、合营企业或联营企业获得的股利

14. 在 2008 年 5 月发布《在子公司、共同控制主体或联营企业中的投资的成本》

---

① 2011 年 5 月，理事会发布的《国际财务报告准则第 13 号——公允价值计量》中包括了公允价值计量的要求。

② 2011 年 5 月，理事会发布的《国际财务报告准则第 13 号——公允价值计量》中包括了公允价值计量的要求。

之前，《国际会计准则第 27 号》提出的是“成本法”。该方法只允许主体将来源于并购后留存收益的分配确认为收益。获得的分配超过留存收益的部分被视为投资成本的收回，应冲减投资成本。在单独财务报表首次采用国际财务报告准则时，为追溯应用这一方法，投资者需要知道子公司在被并购前按照国际财务报告准则核算产生的留存收益。

15. 重述并购前的留存收益的难度类似于企业合并的重述（《国际财务报告准则第 1 号——首次采用国际财务报告准则》在其附录三中就此提供了豁免）。这可能涉及主观地运用后见之明，从而降低了信息的相关性和可靠性。在某些情况下，重述可能难度很大并且成本很高。在其他情况下，重述是不可能的（因为可能涉及判断子公司资产或负债在并购日的公允价值）。

16. 因此，在修订《国际财务报告准则第 1 号》的征求意见稿——《在子公司中的投资的成本》（2007 年 1 月发布）中，为适用成本法，理事会建议豁免首次采用者重述并购日子公司的留存收益。

17. 在考虑上述征求意见稿的反馈意见时，理事会注意到，成本法的基础原则是投资取得的收益应冲减投资的账面价值。然而，以前版本的《国际会计准则第 27 号》的措辞在某些国家或地区产生了问题，因为它特别提及留存收益作为判断的基础。理事会决定解决这一问题的最好方法是删除关于成本法的定义。

18. 在删除成本法定义的同时，理事会的结论认为，投资者应当在单独财务报表中将从子公司、合营企业或联营企业获得的股利确认为收益。因此，从国际财务报告准则中删除了关于将留存收益区分为并购前与并购后两部分并以此判断股利是否是相关投资的收回的要求。

19. 为降低因删除成本法定义而导致在单独财务报表中高估在子公司、合营企业或联营企业投资的风险，理事会建议相关的投资应根据《国际会计准则第 36 号——资产减值》的要求进行减值测试。

20. 2007 年 12 月，理事会在征求意见稿《在子公司、共同控制主体或联营企业中的投资的成本》中发布了修订后的建议，该征求意见稿是有关《国际会计准则第 27 号》和《国际财务报告准则第 1 号》的修订建议。反馈意见总体上支持对《国际会计准则第 27 号》的修订建议，关于投资者确认股利并对相关投资进行减值测试的要求除外。根据收到的反馈意见，理事会修改了其建议并且确定了具体的减值迹象缩减了投资者确认股利时需要对相关投资进行减值测试的情形（参见《国际会计准则第 36 号》第 12 段（8））。理事会将这一修订包含在 2008 年 5 月发布的《在子公司、共同控制主体或联营企业中的投资的成本》中。

新母公司单独财务报表中成本的计量

21. 2007 年，理事会收到了关于母公司通过设立新的主体作为其母公司的方式对集团结构进行重组时如何适用第 10 段（1）的征询。新的母公司通过发行权益工具交换原母公司权益工具获得了原母公司的控制权。

22. 在这一类型的重组中，重组前后新集团和原集团的资产和负债完全相同。除此之外，重组后，原集团的所有者对新集团净资产享有的相对和绝对权益与他们在重组前在原集团净资产享有的相对和绝对权益相同。最后，这一类型的重组涉及现存主体及其股东同意在它们之间设立新的母公司。相对而言，大多数形成母子公司关系的交易或事项由母公司发起，将某主体在集团结构中置于其之下。

23. 因此，理事会决定，母公司以上述特定方式设立新母公司这种有限情况下适用第 10 段（1）时，新母公司应当以重组日原母公司单独财务报表中享有的权益项份额的账面价值计量投资成本。2007 年 12 月，理事会发布的修改《国际会计准则第 27 号》的征求意见稿中增加了关于这一要求的段落。

24. 在对收到的反馈意见作出回应时，理事会修改了征求意见稿中建议的修订（第 13 段和和 14 段），以明确上述要求适用于以下类型的重组，如果它们满足建议的修订所提出的条件：

（1）新母公司没有获得原母公司全部权益工具的重组。例如，新母公司发行权益工具交换原母公司的普通股，但是没有获得原母公司的优先股。此外，新母公司获得了原母公司的控制权，但是没有获得原母公司所有的普通股。

（2）在集团内部设立中层母公司，并且设立集团新的最终母公司。

（3）不是母公司的主体建立新的主体作为其母公司的重组。

25. 此外，理事会明确上述修订是集中于资产的计量，即在新母公司单独财务报表中新母公司对原母公司投资。该修订不适用于新母公司或原母公司单独财务报表或合并财务报表中任何其他资产或负债的计量。

26. 理事会将该修订包含在 2008 年 5 月发布的《在子公司、共同控制主体或联营企业中的投资的成本》中。

27. 理事会没有更广泛地考虑其他类型重组或同一控制交易的会计处理。因此，第 13 段和 14 段仅适用于满足这些段落所提条件的情形。因此，理事会希望主体继续按照相应的会计政策处理不满足第 13 段和 14 段条件的交易。理事会计划在未来关于同一控制交易的项目中考虑同一控制的定义和同一控制下企业合并的会计处理。

披露（2011 年修改）

28. 2011 年修改《国际会计准则第 27 号》时，理事会明确了编制单独财务报表的主体的披露要求，以便要求这类主体披露在子公司、合营企业或联营企业中的重大投资的主要业务所在地（和公司注册国，如果不同的话），如果可行的话，还要求披露根据国际财务报告准则编制合并财务报表的母公司重大投资的主要业务所在地（和公司注册国，如果不同的话）。《国际会计准则第 27 号》（2008 年修改）曾要求披露此类主体的公司注册国家或居住地。澄清这一披露要求以与其他国际财务报告准则（如《国际财务报告准则第 12 号》、《国际会计准则第 1 号——财务报表列报》）的要求更好地保持了一致，这些准则也要求披露公司注册国家和主要业务地。

生效日期（2011 年修改）

29. 理事会决定将本准则的生效日期与《国际财务报告准则第 10 号》、《国际财务报告准则第 11 号》、《国际财务报告准则第 12 号》和《国际会计准则第 28 号》（2011 年修改）的生效日期保持一致。在作出这一决定时，理事会注意到，上述五项国际财务报告准则都涉及报告主体与其他主体特定关系（如当报告主体对另一主体具有控制、共同控制或者重大影响时）的评价、相关会计处理和披露要求。因此，理事会得出结论，适用《国际会计准则第 27 号》而不适用其他四项国际财务报告准则将造成不必要的困惑。

30. 理事会通常将生效日期设定在国际财务报告准则发布之后的 12 个月至 18 个月之间。当决定上述五项国际财务报告准则的生效日期时，理事会考虑了下列因素：

（1）许多国家进行翻译并将这些强制要求引入法律所需的时间。

（2）合并报表项目与 2007 年爆发的全球金融危机相关，理事会根据二十国集团领导人、金融稳定理事会、财务报表使用者、监管机构和其他方的紧急要求加速了该项目的进程，以改进主体表外活动的会计处理和披露。

（3）2010 年 10 月发布的《生效日期和过渡方法征询意见》主要涉及 2011 年发布的国际财务报告准则的实施成本、生效日期和过渡性规定。收到的许多反馈意见并不认为关于合并报表和合营企业安排的国际财务报告准则是对其实施所要求的时间和资源具有很大的影响的准则。此外，只要少数反馈意见认为上述国际财务报告准则的生效日期应当与 2011 年发布的其他国际财务报告准则的生效日期保持一致。

31. 鉴于上述提及的因素，理事会决定要求主体在 2013 年 1 月 1 日及以后日期开始的年度期间适用上述五项国际财务报告准则。

32. 许多对《生效日期和过渡方法征询意见》的反馈意见支持提前适用 2011 年发布的国际财务报告准则。这些反馈意见强调，提前适用对于 2011 年和 2012 年的首次采用者尤其重要。理事会认可了这些意见，决定允许提前适用《国际财务报告准则第 27 号》，如果主体同时提前适用其他几项准则（如《国际财务报告准则第 10 号》、《国际财务报告准则第 11 号》、《国际财务报告准则第 12 号》和《国际会计准则第 28 号》（2011 年修改）），以避免财务报表之间缺乏可比性，这与结论基础第 29 段提到的，将这五项国际财务报告准则的生效日期设定为相同日期的原因相同。即使主体同时适用上述五项国际财务报告准则，理事会注意到，这也无法阻止主体更早地提供《国际财务报告准则第 12 号》所要求的信息，如果这样做能使使用者更好地理解主体与其他主体之间的关系。

Mary E Barth 和 Philippe Danjou 对 2008 年 5 月发布的《在子公司、共同控制主体或联营企业中的投资的成本》（对《国际财务报告准则第 1 号》和《国际会计准则第 27 号》的修订）的不同意见

1. Barth 教授和 Danjou 先生投票反对发布《在子公司、共同控制主体或联营企业中的投资的成本》（对《国际财务报告准则第 1 号——首次采用国际财务报告准则》和《国际会计准则第 27 号——合并财务报表和单独财务报表》的修改）。他们反对的原因如下。

2. 这些理事不同意《国际会计准则第 27 号》中第 13 段和第 14 段的要求，即当重组满足这些段落提出的要求并导致新母公司根据《国际会计准则第 27 号》第 10 段（1）的要求以成本计量对原母公司的投资时，新母公司必须将重组日其在原母公司单独财务报表中列示的权益项份额的账面价值作为该成本。

3. 这些理事承认，新母公司可以选择适用《国际会计准则第 27 号》第 10 段（2），按照《国际会计准则第 39 号——金融工具：确认和计量》对其在原母公司投资进行会计处理。然而，要求新母公司在随后的会计期间按照《国际会计准则第 39 号》对该投资进行会计处理，并且同一类别的所有其他投资均应按照《国际会计准则第 39 号》[①] 进行会计处理。

4. 这些理事也承认，如《国际会计准则第 27 号》结论基础第 23 段所述，这一类型的重组不同其他类型重组的原因是，重组前后新集团的资产和负债与原集团完全相同，原母公司的所有者在这些集团净资产中的权益也完全相同。因此，采用之前的账面价值计量新母公司对原母公司的投资成本可能是合理的，因为新母公司的单独财务报表将其财务状况反映为之前存在的集团的一部分。

5. 然而，这些理事认为，这不能禁止新母公司以作为重组一部分而发行的股份的公允价值计量其在原母公司中投资的成本。单独财务报表编制是将母公司反映为一个单独的法律主体（即不将其考虑为集团的一部分）。尽管这类重组不改变集团的资产和负债，并且从新母公司作为一单独法律主体看，不会因此在合并报表层面产生会计影响，但是其状况已经发生了变化，发行了股份并且获得了以前没有的投资。此外，在许多国家或地区，商业法或公司治理规定要求主体以发行股份收到的对价的公允价值计量所发行的新股份。

6. 这些理事认为，新母公司在原公司投资成本的合理计量基础取决于理事会对单独财务报表的看法。理事会正在或将在《概念框架》的报告主体阶段和共同控制交易项目中讨论相关问题。因此，这些理事认为，理事会在报告主体和共同控制交易

---

① 2009 年 11 月和 2010 年 10 月，国际会计准则理事会修改了《国际会计准则第 39 号》的一些要求，并将它们移入《国际财务报告准则第 9 号——金融工具》。《国际财务报告准则第 9 号》适用于所有纳入《国际会计准则第 39 号》范围的项目。

项目对相关问题的讨论完成之前，理事会应允许新母公司以其在原母公司单独财务报表中享有的权益份额的账面价值或其发行权益工具的公允价值计量对原母公司投资的成本。

对照表

下表反映了《国际会计准则第 27 号——合并财务报表与单独财务报表》（被取代的《国际会计准则第 27 号》）的内容与《国际会计准则第 27 号——单独财务报表》内容的对照情况。被取代的《国际会计准则第 27 号》中的一些内容已经包含在《国际财务报告准则第 10 号》和《国际财务报告准则第 12 号》中；下表反映了这些段落的对照情况。即便相关的要求不同，但如果这些段落大体规范了相同的事项，它们可视为相互对应。

被取代的《国际会计准则第 27 号》段落	修订的《国际会计准则第 27 号》段落	《国际财务报告准则第 10 号》段落	《国际财务报告准则第 12 号》段落
1		1	
2		3	
3	2		
4	4，5	附录一	
5			
6－8	6－8		
9		1，2	
10		4（1）	
11			
12		附录一	
13		7	
14		应用指南第 47 段	
15		应用指南第 48 段和第 49 段	
16，17			
18		应用指南第 86 段	
19		应用指南第 89 段	
20，21		应用指南第 86 段（3）	
22，23		应用指南第 92 段和第 93 段	
24		19	
25，26		应用指南第 87 段和第 88 段	
27		22	
28，29		应用指南第 94 段和第 95 段	
30		23	

续表

被取代的《国际会计准则第27号》段落	修订的《国际会计准则第27号》段落	《国际财务报告准则第10号》段落	《国际财务报告准则第12号》段落
31		应用指南第96段	
32		应用指南第83段	
33－35		应用指南第97段至99段	
36		25（2）	
37		25（2）	
38	10		
38A－38C	12－14		
39	3		
40	11		
41			10－19
42，43	16，17		
44－45E	18		
46	20		
None	1，9，15，19		

2011年5月作出的主要改变是《国际财务报告准则第10号——合并财务报表》取代了《国际会计准则第27号》中关于合并报表的要求。只有关于编制单独财务报表的会计处理和披露要求仍包括在《国际会计准则第27号》中；该准则因此重新命名为“单独财务报表”。

International Accounting Standard 27
Separate Financial Statements

CONTENTS

Introduction

IN1 IAS 27 *Separate Financial Statements* contains accounting and disclosure requirements for investments in subsidiaries, joint ventures and associates when an entity prepares separate financial statements. The Standard requires an entity preparing separate financial statements to account for those investments at cost or in accordance with IFRS 9 *Financial Instruments*.

IN2 The Standard is effective for annual periods beginning on or after 1 January 2013. Earlier application is permitted.

International Accounting Standard 27
Separate Financial Statements

Objective

1 The objective of this Standard is to prescribe the accounting and disclosure requirements for investments in subsidiaries, joint ventures and associates when an entity prepares separate financial statements.

Scope

2 **This Standard shall be applied in accounting for investments in subsidiaries, joint ventures and associates when an entity elects, or is required by local regulations, to present separate financial statements.**

3 This Standard does not mandate which entities produce separate financial statements. It applies when an entity prepares separate financial statements that comply with International Financial Reporting Standards.

Definitions

4 **The following terms are used in this Standard with the meanings specified:**

Consolidated financial statements **are the financial statements of a group in which the assets, liabilities, equity, income, expenses and cash flows of the parent and its subsidiaries are presented as those of a single economic entity.**

Separate financial statements **are those presented by a parent (ie an investor with control of a subsidiary) or an investor with joint control of, or significant influence over, an investee, in which the investments are accounted for at cost or in accordance with IFRS 9** ***Financial Instruments*****.**

5 The following terms are defined in Appendix A of IFRS 10 *Consolidated Financial Statements*, Appendix A of IFRS 11 *Joint Arrangements* and paragraph 3 of IAS 28 *Investments in Associates and Joint Ventures*:

- associate
- control of an investee
- group

- joint control
- joint venture
- joint venturer
- parent
- significant influence
- subsidiary.

6 Separate financial statements are those presented in addition to consolidated financial statements or in addition to financial statements in which investments in associates or joint ventures are accounted for using the equity method, other than in the circumstances set out in paragraph 8. Separate financial statements need not be appended to, or accompany, those statements.

7 Financial statements in which the equity method is applied are not separate financial statements. Similarly, the financial statements of an entity that does not have a subsidiary, associate or joint venturer's interest in a joint venture are not separate financial statements.

8 An entity that is exempted in accordance with paragraph 4 (a) of IFRS 10 from consolidation or paragraph 17 of IAS 28 (as amended in 2011) from applying the equity method may present separate financial statements as its only financial statements.

Preparation of separate financial statements

9 Separate financial statements shall be prepared in accordance with all applicable IFRSs, except as provided in paragraph 10.

10 When an entity prepares separate financial statements, it shall account for investments in subsidiaries, joint ventures and associates either:

(a) at cost, or

(b) in accordance with IFRS 9.

The entity shall apply the same accounting for each category of investments. Investments accounted for at cost shall be accounted for in accordance withIFRS 5 *Non-current Assets Held for Sale and Discontinued Operations* when they are classified as held for sale (or included in a disposal group that is classified as held

for sale). The measurement of investments accounted for in accordance with IFRS 9 is not changed in such circumstances.

11 If an entity elects, in accordance with paragraph 18 of IAS 28 (as amended in 2011), to measure its investments in associates or joint ventures at fair value through profit or loss in accordance with IFRS 9, it shall also account for those investments in the same way in its separate financial statements.

12 An entity shall recognise a dividend from a subsidiary, a joint venture or an associate in profit or loss in its separate financial statements when its right to receive the dividend is established.

13 When a parent reorganises the structure of its group by establishing a new entity as its parent in a manner that satisfies the following criteria:

(a) the new parent obtains control of the original parent by issuing equity instruments in exchange for existing equity instruments of the original parent;

(b) the assets and liabilities of the new group and the original group are the same immediately before and after the reorganisation; and

(c) the owners of the original parent before the reorganisation have the same absolute and relative interests in the net assets of the original group and the new group immediately before and after the reorganisation,

and the new parent accounts for its investment in the original parent in accordance with paragraph 10(a) in its separate financial statements, the new parent shall measure cost at the carrying amount of its share of the equity items shown in the separate financial statements of the original parent at the date of the reorganisation.

14 Similarly, an entity that is not a parent might establish a new entity as its parent in a manner that satisfies the criteria in paragraph 13. The requirements in paragraph 13 apply equally to such reorganisations. In such cases, references to 'original parent' and 'original group' are to the 'original entity'.

Disclosure

15 An entity shall apply all applicable IFRSs when providing disclosures in its separate financial statements, including the requirements in paragraphs 16 and 17.

16 When a parent, in accordance with paragraph 4(a) of IFRS 10, elects not to

prepare consolidated financial statements and instead prepares separate financial statements, it shall disclose in those separate financial statements:

(a) the fact that the financial statements are separate financial statements; that the exemption from consolidation has been used; the name and principal place of business (and country of incorporation, if different) of the entity whose consolidated financial statements that comply with International Financial Reporting Standards have been produced for public use; and the address where those consolidated financial statements are obtainable.

(b) a list of significant investments in subsidiaries, joint ventures and associates, including:

(i) the name of those investees.

(ii) the principal place of business (and country of incorporation, if different) of those investees.

(iii) its proportion of the ownership interest (and its proportion of the voting rights, if different) held in those investees.

(c) a description of the method used to account for the investments listed under (b).

17 **When a parent (other than a parent covered by paragraph 16) or an investor with joint control of, or significant influence over, an investee prepares separate financial statements, the parent or investor shall identify the financial statements prepared in accordance with IFRS 10, IFRS 11 or IAS 28 (as amended in 2011) to which they relate. The parent or investor shall also disclose in its separate financial statements:**

(a) the fact that the statements are separate financial statements and the reasons why those statements are prepared if not required by law.

(b) a list of significant investments in subsidiaries, joint ventures and associates, including:

(i) the name of those investees.

(ii) the principal place of business (and country of incorporation, if different) of those investees.

(iii) its proportion of the ownership interest (and its proportion of the

voting rights, if different) held in those investees.

(c) a description of the method used to account for the investments listed under (b).

The parent or investor shall also identify the financial statements prepared in accordance withIFRS 10, IFRS 11 or IAS 28 (as amended in 2011) to which they relate.

Effective date and transition

18 An entity shall apply this Standard for annual periods beginning on or after 1 January 2013. Earlier application is permitted. If an entity applies this Standard earlier, it shall disclose that fact and apply IFRS 10, IFRS 11 , IFRS 12 *Disclosure of Interests in Other Entities* and IAS 28 (as amended in 2011) at the same time.

References to IFRS 9

19 If an entity applies this Standard but does not yet apply IFRS 9, any reference to IFRS 9 shall be read as a reference to IAS 39 *Financial Instruments: Recognition and Measurement*.

Withdrawal of IAS 27 (2008)

20 This Standard is issued concurrently with IFRS 10. Together, the two IFRSs supersede IAS 27 *Consolidated and Separate Financial Statements* (as amended in 2008).

Approval by the Board of IAS 27 issued in December 2003

International Accounting Standard 27 *Consolidated and Separate Financial Statements* (as revised in 2003) was approved for issue by thirteen of the fourteen members of the International Accounting Standards Board. Mr Yamada dissented. His dissenting opinion related to consolidated financial statements and is set out after the Basis for Conclusions on IFRS 10 *Consolidated Financial Statements*.

Sir David Tweedie	Chairman
Thomas E Jones	Vice-Chairman
Mary E Barth	
Hans-Georg Bruns	
Anthony T Cope	
Robert P Garnett	
Gilbert Gélard	
James J Leisenring	
Warren J McGregor	
Patricia L O' Malley	
Harry K Schmid	
John T Smith	
Geoffrey Whittington	
Tatsumi Yamada	

Approval by the Board of *Cost of an Investment in a Subsidiary, Jointly Controlled Entity or Associate* (Amendments to IFRS 1 and IAS 27) issued in May 2008

Cost of an Investment in a Subsidiary, Jointly Controlled Entity or Associate (Amendments to IFRS 1 *First-time Adoption of International Financial Reporting Standards* and IAS 27) was approved for issue by eleven of the thirteen members of the International Accounting Standards Board. Professor Barth and Mr Danjou dissented. Their dissenting opinions are set out after the Basis for Conclusions.

Sir David Tweedie	Chairman
Thomas E Jones	Vice-Chairman
Mary E Barth	
Stephen Cooper	
Philippe Danjou	
Jan Engström	
Robert P Garnett	
Gilbert Gélard	
James J Leisenring	
Warren J McGregor	
John T Smith	
Tatsumi Yamada	
Wei-Guo Zhang	

Basis for Conclusions on IAS 27 *Separate Financial Statements*

This Basis for Conclusions accompanies, but is not part of, IAS 27.

Introduction

BC1 This Basis for Conclusions summarises the International Accounting Standards Board's considerations in reaching its conclusions on issuing IAS 27 *Consolidated and Separate Financial Statements* in 2003, and amending IAS 27 in 2008 and again in 2011. Individual Board members gave greater weight to some factors than to others. Unless otherwise noted, references below to IAS 27 are to previous versions of the Standard.

BC2 The amendment of IAS 27 in 2011 resulted from the Board's project on consolidation. A new IFRS, IFRS 10 *Consolidated Financial Statements*, addresses the principle of control and requirements relating to the preparation of consolidated financial statements. As a result, IAS 27 now contains requirements relating only to separate financial statements. This change is reflected in the Standard's amended title, *Separate Financial Statements*.

BC3 In approving the publication of IFRS 10 in 2011, the Board also approved consequential amendments to IAS 27 that removed from the Standard all requirements relating to consolidated financial statements.

BC4 At the same time, the Board relocated to IAS 27 requirements from IAS 28 *Investments in Associates* and IAS 31 *Interests in Joint Ventures* regarding separate financial statements. Those requirements are in paragraphs 6-8 of the Standard. Given the extent of the material that has been removed or relocated, the Board decided, for clarity, to renumber the paragraphs in the amended IAS 27. The definitions and wording in the Standard were also updated to be consistent with the requirements in IFRS 10, IFRS 11 *Joint Arrangements*, IFRS 12 *Disclosure of Interests in Other Entities*, and IAS 28 *Investments in Associates and Joint Ventures*.

BC5 When issued in 2003, IAS 27 was accompanied by a Basis for Conclusions summarising the considerations of the Board, as constituted at the time, in reaching its conclusions. The Basis for Conclusions was subsequently updated to reflect amendments to the Standard.

BC6 This Basis for Conclusions now includes only the Board's considerations on separate financial statements. Cross-references have been updated accordingly and minor necessary editorial changes have been made. The paragraphs discussing consolidated financial statements have been relocated to the Basis for Conclusions on IFRS 10 as appropriate.

Consolidation exemption available for non-public entities

BC7 The Board decided that a parent that meets the criteria in paragraph 4(a) of IFRS 10 for exemption from the requirement to prepare consolidated financial statements should, in its separate financial statements, account for those subsidiaries in the same way as other parents, joint venturers with interests in joint ventures or investors in associates account for investments in their separate financial statements. The Board draws a distinction between accounting for such investments as equity investments and accounting for the economic entity that the parent controls. In relation to the former, the Board decided that each category of investment should be accounted for consistently.

BC8 The Board decided that the same approach to accounting for investments in separate financial statements should apply irrespective of the circumstances for which they are prepared. Thus, a parent that presents consolidated financial statements, and a parent that does not because it is exempted, should present the same form of separate financial statements.

Measurement of investments in subsidiaries, joint ventures and associates in separate financial statements (2003 revision and 2008 amendments)

BC9 IAS 27 (as revised by the Board's predecessor body in 2000) permitted entities to measure investments in subsidiaries in any one of three ways in the parent's separate financial statements. These were at cost, using the equity method, or as available-for-sale[①] financial assets in accordance with IAS 39 *Financial Instruments: Recognition and Measurement*.[②] IAS 28 *Investments in Associates* permitted the same choices for investments in associates in separate financial statements, and IAS 31 *Interests in Joint Ventures* stated that IAS 31 did not indicate a preference for any particular treatment for accounting for interests in joint ventures in a joint venturer's separate financial statements. However, in 2003 the Board decided to require the use of cost or IAS 39 for all investments included in separate financial statements and to remove the equity method as one of the measurement options.

① IFRS 9 *Financial Instruments*, issued in November 2009 and amended in October 2010, eliminated the category of available-for-sale financial assets.

② In November 2009 and October 2010 the IASB amended some of the requirements of IAS 39 and relocated them to IFRS 9 *Financial Instruments*. IFRS 9 applies to all items within the scope of IAS 39.

BC10 Although the equity method would provide users with some profit or loss information similar to that obtained from consolidation, the Board noted that such information is reflected in the investor's consolidated or individual financial statements and does not need to be provided to the users of its separate financial statements. For separate financial statements, the focus is upon the performance of the assets as investments. The Board concluded that separate financial statements prepared using either the fair value method in accordance with IAS 39① or the cost method would be relevant. Using the fair value method in accordance with IAS 39 would provide a measure of the economic value of the investments. Using the cost method can result in relevant information, depending on the purpose of preparing the separate financial statements. For example, they may be needed only by particular parties to determine the dividend income from subsidiaries.

BC11 As part of its annual improvements project begun in 2007, the Board identified an apparent inconsistency with IFRS 5 *Non-current Assets Held For Sale and Discontinued Operations*. The inconsistency related to the accounting by a parent in its separate financial statements when investments it accounts for in accordance with IAS 39 are classified as held for sale in accordance with IFRS 5. Paragraph 10 requires an entity that prepares separate financial statements to account for such investments that are classified as held for sale (or included in a disposal group that is classified as held for sale) in accordance with IFRS 5 if they are measured at cost. However, financial assets that an entity accounts for in accordance with IAS 39 are excluded from IFRS 5's measurement requirements.

BC12 Paragraph BC13 of the Basis for Conclusions on IFRS 5 explains that the Board decided that non-current assets should be excluded from the measurement scope of IFRS 5 only 'if (i) they are already carried at fair value with changes in fair value recognised in profit or loss or (ii) there would be difficulties in determining their fair value less costs to sell.'② The Board acknowledged in the Basis for Conclusions on IFRS 5 that not all financial assets within the scope of IAS 39 are recognised at fair value with changes in fair value recognised in profit or loss, but it did not want to make any further changes to the accounting for financial assets at that time.

BC13 Therefore, the Board amended paragraph 10 by *Improvements to IFRSs* issued in May 2008 to align the accounting in separate financial statements for those investments that

---

① In May 2011 the Board issued IFRS 13 *Fair Value Measurement*, which contains requirements for measuring fair value.

② In May 2011 the Board issued IFRS 13 *Fair Value Measurement*, which contains requirements for measuring fair value.

are accounted for in accordance with IAS 39 with the measurement exclusion that IFRS 5 provides for other assets that are accounted for in accordance with IAS 39 before classification as held for sale. Thus, an entity should continue to account for such investments in accordance with IAS 39 when they meet the held for sale criteria in IFRS 5.

Dividend received from a subsidiary, a joint venture or an associate

BC14 Before *Cost of an Investment in a Subsidiary, Jointly Controlled Entity or Associate* was issued in May 2008, IAS 27 described a 'cost method'. This required an entity to recognise distributions as income only if they came from post-acquisition retained earnings. Distributions received in excess of such retained earnings were regarded as a recovery of investment and were recognised as a reduction in the cost of the investment. To apply that method retrospectively upon first-time adoption of IFRSs in its separate financial statements, an investor would need to know the subsidiary's pre-acquisition retained earnings in accordance with IFRSs.

BC15 Restating pre-acquisition retained earnings would be a task tantamount to restating the business combination (for which IFRS 1 *First-time Adoption of International Financial Reporting Standards* provides an exemption in Appendix C). It might involve subjective use of hindsight, which would diminish the relevance and reliability of the information. In some cases, the restatement would be time-consuming and difficult. In other cases, it would be impossible (because it would involve making judgements about the fair values of the assets and liabilities of a subsidiary at the acquisition date).

BC16 Therefore, in *Cost of an Investment in a Subsidiary*, an exposure draft of proposed amendments to IFRS 1 (published in January 2007), the Board proposed to give first-time adopters an exemption from restating the retained earnings of the subsidiary at the date of acquisition for the purpose of applying the cost method.

BC17 In considering the responses to that exposure draft, the Board observed that the principle underpinning the cost method is that a return of an investment should be deducted from the carrying amount of the investment. However, the wording in the previous version of IAS 27 created a problem in some jurisdictions because it made specific reference to retained earnings as the means of making that assessment. The Board decided that the best way to resolve this issue was to delete the definition of the cost method.

BC18 In removing the definition of the cost method, the Board concluded that an investor should recognise a dividend from a subsidiary, a joint venture or an associate as income in its separate financial statements. Consequently, the requirement to separate the retained earnings of an entity into pre-acquisition and post-acquisition components as a method for assessing whether a dividend is a recovery of its associated investment has been removed from IFRSs.

BC19 To reduce the risk that removing the definition of the cost method would lead to investments in subsidiaries, joint ventures and associates being overstated in the separate financial statements of the investor, the Board proposed that the related investment should be tested for impairment in accordance with IAS 36 *Impairment of Assets*.

BC20 The Board published its revised proposals in *Cost of an Investment in a Subsidiary, Jointly Controlled Entity or Associate* , an exposure draft of proposed amendments to IFRS 1 and IAS 27, in December 2007. Respondents generally supported the proposed amendments to IAS 27, except for the proposal to require impairment testing of the related investment when an investor recognises a dividend. In the light of the comments received, the Board revised its proposal and identified specific indicators of impairment. This was done to narrow the circumstances in which impairment testing of the related investment would be required when an investor recognises a dividend (see paragraph 12 (h) of IAS 36). The Board included the amendments in *Cost of an Investment in a Subsidiary, Jointly Controlled Entity or Associate* issued in May 2008.

Measurement of cost in the separate financial statements of a new parent

BC21 In 2007 the Board received enquiries about the application of paragraph 10(a) when a parent reorganises the structure of its group by establishing a new entity as its parent. The new parent obtains control of the original parent by issuing equity instruments in exchange for existing equity instruments of the original parent.

BC22 In this type of reorganisation, the assets and liabilities of the new group and the original group are the same immediately before and after the reorganisation. In addition, the owners of the original parent have the same relative and absolute interests in the net assets of the new group immediately after the reorganisation as they had in the net assets of the original group before the reorganisation. Finally, this type of reorganisation involves an existing entity and its shareholders agreeing to create a new parent between them. In contrast, many transactions or events that result in a parent-subsidiary relationship are initiated by a parent over an entity that will be positioned below it in the structure of the group.

BC23 Therefore, the Board decided that in applying paragraph 10 (a) *in the limited circumstances in which a parent establishes a new parent in this particular manner*, the new parent should measure the cost of its investment in the original parent at the carrying amount of its share of the equity items shown in the separate financial statements of the original parent at the date of the reorganisation. In December 2007 the Board published an exposure draft proposing to amend IAS 27 to add a paragraph with that requirement.

BC24 In response to comments received from respondents to that exposure draft, the Board modified the drafting of the amendment (paragraphs 13 and 14) to clarify that it applies to the following types of reorganisations when they satisfy the criteria specified in the amendment:

(a) reorganisations in which the new parent does not acquire all the equity instruments of the original parent. For example, a new parent might issue equity instruments in exchange for ordinary shares of the original parent, but not acquire the preference shares of the original parent. In addition, a new parent might obtain control of the original parent, but not acquire all the ordinary shares of the original parent.

(b) the establishment of an intermediate parent within a group, as well as the establishment of a new ultimate parent of a group.

(c) reorganisations in which an entity that is not a parent establishes a new entity as its parent.

BC25 In addition, the Board clarified that the amendment focuses on the measurement of one asset—the new parent's investment in the original parent in the new parent's separate financial statements. The amendment does not apply to the measurement of any other assets or liabilities in the separate financial statements of either the original parent or the new parent or in the consolidated financial statements.

BC26 The Board included the amendment in *Cost of an Investment in a Subsidiary, Jointly Controlled Entity or Associate* issued in May 2008.

BC27 The Board did not consider the accounting for other types of reorganisations or for common control transactions more broadly. Accordingly, paragraphs 13 and 14 apply only when the criteria in those paragraphs are satisfied. Therefore, the Board expects that entities would continue to account for transactions that do not satisfy the criteria in paragraphs 13 and 14 in accordance with their accounting policies for such transactions. The Board plans to consider the definition of common control and the accounting for business combinations under common control in a future project on common control transactions.

Disclosure (2011 amendments)

BC28 When IAS 27 was amended in 2011, the Board clarified the disclosures required by an entity preparing separate financial statements so that the entity would be required to disclose the principal place of business (and country of incorporation, if different) of significant investments in subsidiaries, joint ventures and associates and, if applicable, of the parent that prepares consolidated financial statements that comply with IFRSs. IAS 27 (as amended in 2008) had previously required the disclosure of the country of incorporation or residence of such entities. The clarification of the disclosure requirement is more consistent with those requirements in other IFRSs (eg IFRS 12 and IAS 1 *Presentation of Financial Statements*) that also require disclosure of the principal place of business and country of incorporation.

Effective date (2011 amendments)

BC29 The Board decided to align the effective date for the Standard with the effective date for IFRS 10, IFRS 11, IFRS 12 and IAS 28 (as amended in 2011). When making this decision, the Board noted that the five IFRSs all deal with the assessment of, and related accounting and disclosure requirements about, a reporting entity's special relationships with other entities (ie when the reporting entity has control or joint control of, or significant influence over, another entity). As a result, the Board concluded that applying IAS 27 without also applying the other four IFRSs could cause unwarranted confusion.

BC30 The Board usually sets an effective date of between twelve and eighteen months after issuing an IFRS. When deciding the effective date for the five IFRSs, the Board considered the following factors:

(a) the time that many countries require for translation and for introducing the mandatory requirements into law.

(b) the consolidation project was related to the global financial crisis that started in 2007 and was accelerated by the Board in response to urgent requests from the leaders of the G20, the Financial Stability Board, users of financial statements, regulators and others to improve the accounting and disclosure of an entity's 'off balance sheet' activities.

(c) the comments received from respondents to the Request for Views *Effective Date and Transition Methods* that was published in October 2010 regarding implementation costs, effective date and transition requirements of the IFRSs to be issued in 2011. Most respondents did not identify the consolidation and joint arrangements IFRSs as having a high impact in terms of the time and resources that their implementation would require. In addition, only a few respondents commented that the effective dates of those IFRSs should be aligned with those of the other IFRSs to be issued in 2011.

BC31 With these factors in mind, the Board decided to require entities to apply the five IFRSs for annual periods beginning on or after 1 January 2013.

BC32 Most respondents to the Request for Views supported early application of the IFRSs to be issued in 2011. Respondents stressed that early application was especially important for first-time adopters in 2011 and 2012. The Board was persuaded by these arguments and decided to permit early application of IAS 27 but only if an entity applies it in conjunction with the other IFRSs (ie IFRS 10, IFRS 11, IFRS 12 and IAS 28 (as amended in 2011)) to avoid a lack of comparability among financial statements, and for the reasons noted in paragraph BC29 that triggered the Board's decision to set the same effective date for all five IFRSs. Even though an entity should apply the five IFRSs at the same time, the Board noted that an entity should not be prevented from providing any information required by IFRS 12 early if by doing so users gained a better understanding of the entity's relationships with other entities.

DISSENTING OPINION

Dissent of Mary E Barth and Philippe Danjou from *Cost of an Investment in a Subsidiary, Jointly Controlled Entity or Associate* (Amendments to IFRS 1 and IAS 27) issued in May 2008

Cross-references have been updated.

DO1 Professor Barth and Mr Danjou voted against the publication of *Cost of an Investment in a Subsidiary, Jointly Controlled Entity or Associate* (Amendments to IFRS 1 *First-time Adoption of International Financial Reporting Standards* and IAS 27 *Consolidated and Separate Financial Statements*). The reasons for their dissent are set out below.

DO2 These Board members disagree with the requirement in paragraphs 13 and 14 of IAS 27 that when a reorganisation satisfies the criteria specified in those paragraphs and the resulting new parent accounts for its investment in the original parent at cost in accordance with paragraph 10(a) of IAS 27, the new parent must measure the cost at the carrying amount of its share of the equity items shown in the separate financial statements of the original parent at the date of the reorganisation.

DO3 These Board members acknowledge that a new parent could choose to apply paragraph 10 (b) of IAS 27 and account for its investment in the original parent in accordance with IAS 39 *Financial Instruments: Recognition and Measurement*. However, the new parent then would be required to account for the investment in accordance with IAS 39 in subsequent periods and to account for all other investments in the same category in accordance with IAS 39. ①

DO4 These Board members also acknowledge, as outlined in paragraph BC23 of the Basis for Conclusions on IAS 27, that this type of reorganisation is different from other types of reorganisations in that the assets and liabilities of the new group and the original group are the same immediately before and after the reorganisation, as are the interests of the owners of the original parent in the net assets of those groups. Therefore, using the previous carrying amount to measure the cost of the new parent's investment in the original parent might be appropriate on the basis that the separate financial statements of the new parent would reflect its position as part of a pre-existing group.

---

① In November 2009 and October 2010 the IASB amended some of the requirements of IAS 39 and relocated them to IFRS 9 *Financial Instruments*. IFRS 9 applies to all items within the scope of IAS 39.

DO5 However, these Board members believe that it is inappropriate to preclude a new parent from measuring the cost of its investment in the original parent at the fair value of the shares that it issues as part of the reorganisation. Separate financial statements are prepared to reflect the parent as a separate legal entity (ie not considering that the entity might be part of a group). Although such a reorganisation does not change the assets and liabilities of the group and therefore should have no accounting effect at the consolidated level, from the perspective of the new parent as a separate legal entity, its position has changed—it has issued shares and acquired an investment that it did not have previously. Also, in many jurisdictions, commercial law or corporate governance regulations require entities to measure new shares that they issue at the fair value of the consideration received for the shares.

DO6 These Board members believe that the appropriate measurement basis for the new parent's cost of its investment in the original parent depends on the Board's view of separate financial statements. The Board is or will be discussing related issues in the reporting entity phase of its Conceptual Framework project and in its project on common control transactions. Accordingly, these Board members believe that the Board should have permitted a new parent to measure the cost of its investment in the original parent either at the carrying amount of its share of the equity items shown in the separate financial statements of the original parent or at the fair value of the equity instruments that it issues until the Board discusses the related issues in its projects on reporting entity and common control transactions.

TABLE OF CONCORDANCE

This table shows how the contents of IAS 27 *Consolidated and Separate Financial Statements* (the 'superseded IAS 27') and IAS 27 *Separate Financial Statements* (the 'amended IAS 27') correspond. Some requirements in the superseded version of IAS 27 were incorporated into IFRS 10 and IFRS 12; this table also shows how those paragraphs correspond. Paragraphs are treated as corresponding if they broadly address the same matter even though the requirements may differ.

Superseded IAS 27 paragraph	Amended IAS 27 paragraph	IFRS 10 paragraph	IFRS 12 paragraph
1		1	
2		3	
3	2		
4	4, 5	Appendix A	
5			
6-8	6-8		
9		1, 2	
10		4(a)	
11			
12		Appendix A	
13		7	
14		B47	
15		B48, B49	
16, 17			
18		B86	
19		B89	
20, 21		B86(c)	
22, 23		B92, B93	
24		19	
25, 26		B87, B88	

Superseded IAS 27 paragraph	Amended IAS 27 paragraph	IFRS 10 paragraph	IFRS 12 paragraph
27		22	
28, 29		B94, B95	
30		23	
31		B96	
32		B83	
33-35		B97-B99	
36		25(b)	
37		25(b)	
38	10		
38A-38C	12-14		
39	3		
40	11		
41			10-19
42, 43	16, 17		
44-45E	18		
46	20		
None	1, 9, 15, 19		

The main change made in May 2011 was that IFRS 10 *Consolidated Financial Statements* replaced the consolidation requirements in IAS 27. Only accounting and disclosure requirements for the preparation of separate financial statements remained in IAS 27; the Standard was therefore renamed *Separate Financial Statements*.

